MAKE THE CALL
A 40-DAY EXPERIENCE FOR MEN
MARK RICHT

Lifeway Press®
Nashville, Tennessee

Editorial Team

Susan Hill
Content Developer

Reid Patton
Content Editor

Jon Rodda
Art Director

Joel Polk
Editorial Team Leader

Brian Daniel
Manager, Adult Discipleship Publishing

Brandon Hiltibidal
Director, Adult Ministry

ISBN 978-1-0877-4215-1 • Item 005831519
Dewey Decimal 248.842

Subject headings:
MEN / CHRISTIAN LIFE / BIBLE--STUDY AND TEACHING

Unless otherwise noted, all Scripture quotations are taken from the Christian Standard Bible®, Copyright © 2017 by Holman Bible Publishers. Used by permission. Christian Standard Bible® and CSB® are federally registered trademarks of Holman Bible Publishers.

Scripture quotations taken from the New American Standard Bible® (NASB), Copyright © 1960, 1962, 1963, 1968, 1971, 1972, 1973, 1975, 1977, 1995 by The Lockman Foundation. Used by permission. www.lockman.org.

To order additional copies of this resource, write to Lifeway Resources Customer Service; One Lifeway Plaza; Nashville, TN 37234; fax 615-251-5933; call toll free 800-458-2772; order online at lifeway.com; or email orderentry@lifeway.com. Printed in the United States of America

Adult Ministry Publishing
Lifeway Resources • One Lifeway Plaza • Nashville, TN 37234

Printed in China

TABLE OF CONTENTS

ABOUT THE AUTHOR

Mark Richt is the former head football coach of the University of Georgia Bulldogs and University of Miami Hurricanes, and is currently a football analyst for the ACC Network. He and his wife Katharyn are the parents of four children, and live in Florida.

HOW TO USE

Daily Devotion

This journal provides an 8-week guided experience for men to explore what it means to Make the Call as it relates to godly living. Each week is divided into five days of personal study with three questions at the end of each day's reading.

Group Experience

At the end of each week's study, if you choose, you'll have the opportunity to discuss what you've learned in a group setting. Each guide includes a paragraph summarizing the week's content and a few questions to guide a discussion between a small group of men.

THE EARLY YEARS

DAY 1

*In him you also were sealed with the
promised Holy Spirit when you heard
the word of truth, the gospel of your
salvation, and when you believed.*

EPHESIANS 1:13

MAKE THE CALL

Before I tell you a little about my playing days, let me tell you a story from my later years as a coach. Miami hadn't beaten Florida State in seven years. The year before, at home, we'd come close to beating them. It was October 7, 2017. My second year as head coach in Coral Gables, and my first trip back to Tallahassee as the enemy. This was special to me. At 3:30 in the afternoon, at kickoff under bright sunlight on Bobby Bowden Field, at Doak Campbell Stadium, this was our chance to prove that the U was worthy of the nation's attention once again.

The year before, at home, we'd come close to beating them, close to at least pushing the game into overtime, but things didn't go our way. And this year—man, this year, it looked like they'd gotten us again. The score—Florida State 20, Miami 17. Time remaining on the clock—1:24. Still, we were able to move into field goal range in the final minute. We could tie it. Or … we could go for the win.

In my headset, coaches were giving me their opinions, feeding me up-top observations about what they could see and had seen from the coaches' booth—information and advice that might affect the pros and cons of the various alternatives in front of me. That's what I wanted. That's what I'd asked them for. Then somebody—whoever it was, I can't remember—somebody said, "Make the call, Coach."

That's the thing about making calls. Sometimes you've got to decide. Right now. You don't have a week or ten days to mull it over. But whether you've got all the time in the world to sit and pray about it, or you've got about forty seconds, like I did—you've got to be the one to do it. To make the call.

As Christians, we can be confident in our ability to make decisions—we have what it takes to make the call. The Bible teaches that the Holy Spirit lives in everyone who belongs to Christ (Romans 8:9). The Spirit functions in a number of ways—including filling the role as our Teacher and Guide. When Jesus told His disciples about the Holy Spirit He said, "But the Counselor, the Holy Spirit, whom the Father will send in my name, will teach you all things and remind you of everything I have told you" (John 14:26).

When the Holy Spirit lives inside us, we can move forward knowing He will give us wisdom. And even when we get off-track or make the wrong decision, the Holy Spirit will redirect us on the right path.

When it's time to "make the call," who do you consult or seek out for advice?

How do you grow in your ability to "make the call"?

Which areas of your life would you like to grow in knowledge and wisdom?

DAY 2

*Then Jesus said to his disciples,
"If anyone wants to follow after me,
let him deny himself, take up his cross,
and follow me. For whoever wants to
save his life will lose it, but whoever
loses his life because of me will find it.*

MATTHEW 16:24-25

ALL IN

You may not know this, but I was a quarterback. Actually, a pretty good one. At one point in my career, some considered me the fourth-best quarterback in the nation. Or maybe it was just my mom who thought that. I ended up in South Florida as a thirteen-year-old kid who loved playing ball. And though baseball was my favorite sport, there was just always something about football. I found my identity in football, and it was how I defined what mattered to me.

So when Coach Roger Coffey, head football coach at Boca Raton High, told me prior to my junior year that he wanted me at quarterback, and that if I'd focus on only one sport—no more baseball—he could train me to be good enough to earn a scholarship to play football in college, there was no decision to make. I was football-only from that time forward. If I was going to excel at football it would demand focus.

There are some things in life that require our full attention—our faith is one of them. When we make a decision to follow Christ, He asks that we go "all in." Following Jesus calls for focus and undivided attention. You can't half-heartedly follow Jesus.

Jesus told His disciples, "If anyone wants to follow after me, let him deny himself, take up his cross, and follow me. For whoever wants to save his life will lose it, but whoever loses his life because of me will find it" (Matt. 16:24-25).

When we "deny ourselves," it doesn't mean that we give up everything that brings us enjoyment. God intends for us to live full and meaningful lives (John 10:10). Denying ourselves means we give up the things that hinder us from doing the will of God. As Christ-followers, we align our lives with the truths taught in Scripture. Following Jesus demands we align our will with His. When we "take up our cross," we give our whole life to God—not part of our life—our whole life. In doing so, we find the life we were intended to live all along—the life God created us for.

Describe your faith in this season of your life.

What reservations do you have about "denying yourself" or "taking up your cross?"

What steps can you take to go "all in" as you follow Jesus?

DAY 3

*They devoted themselves to the apostles'
teaching, to the fellowship, to the
breaking of bread, and to prayer.*

ACTS 2:42

THE VALUE OF COMMUNITY

I remember Coach Coffey asking me one time if I believed in God. I'm not sure why he asked me that. Maybe he sensed my priorities were out of whack. "I don't know, Coach," I said, "but I'll tell you what I do believe in. I believe in football."

I thought he'd be proud of that. But the look on his face wasn't the look of approval I expected. He didn't really say anything. In hindsight, maybe he thought he'd created a monster.

I learned so much from Coach Coffey. He taught me how to be a quarterback. He coached me not just on the practice field and in the classroom but in his home, in his life. I spent a lot of time at his house as a high-school kid—eating meals, watching game film, just hanging out with his family. One of his daughters, no joke, still calls me her brother.

Coach Coffey was the type of coach who made young men out of football players. He had a rule for us: if any trouble ever broke out at the school, which was always a possibility, we were to head straight for the cafeteria and meet him there. If you wanted to be on his team, that's where you better be. No fighting. No trouble. I loved him. I'd have done anything for him.

In football, you quickly learn the value of coaches, mentors, and the greater sports community. We learn from one another and need each other. It's the same way in Christian community. You need mature people in the faith to teach and guide you. And you need to use what you've learned to mentor those who came to faith later than you. You need brothers and sisters in Christ who spend time with you and your family. There are no spiritual hermits in the Bible—the Christian life is meant to be lived in community.

Who do you seek for spiritual guidance?

Are you mentoring anyone? Who do you know who could use a friend?

What steps can you take to get more involved in a community centered around faith?

DAY 4

When you pass through the waters,
I will be with you, and the rivers will
not overwhelm you. When you walk
through the fire, you will not be scorched,
and the flame will not burn you.

ISAIAH 43:2

AN IDENTITY CRISIS

At Boca High, you pretty much fit into one of three peer groups. You were either a nerd, a jock, or a surfer. Not really, but in general. I was a jock. A jock who was going places. A jock they'd all be talking about one day.

I was a guy who believed in football.

But what I didn't know was, it's a big problem if your identity is all wrapped up in what you do rather than who you are. When your identity is in what you do, and when what you do falls apart, YOU fall apart.

But the God I wasn't sure I believed in—the God who knew exactly what to do with a guy who believed only in football—must have decided the time was right for taking me through a crisis of identity. He did it by letting me watch Jim Kelly live out my dreams.

This was the guy I would forever be backing up. He wasn't going to be leaving his seat unoccupied anytime soon. We were in the same class. Barring injury, I knew I wouldn't be seeing much playing time. However, Jim did get hurt our senior season, so I got to play in five games. But by then, I'd already thrown most of my drive and determination away. Instead of being All-American on the field, I'd become All-American at the nighttime games. All those big-time hopes and dreams of mine were gone. Blown out of the water. And yet it was my identity that had taken the biggest beating of all.

There are times when God allows us to go through seasons of hardship to reveal our need for Him. I had been attempting to build my identity through my performance and when things didn't go the way I'd planned, I had to reassess who I was. At the time, I had no way of knowing that God was using my circumstances to work on my heart and make me see my need for Him. I didn't know it yet, but I would learn that when we place our identity in what we do or how we perform, our self-worth can easily be crushed. But when we realize our value is already established because we are a child of God—that can't be taken from us.

**In a few words, how would you describe yourself?
What makes you valuable?**

**Would your identity change if you were no longer able
to perform your job? Why or why not?**

**How does your relationship with God affect the way
you view your identity?**

DAY 5

*Indeed, we have all received grace
upon grace from his fullness*

JOHN 1:16

CONTAGIOUS FAITH

The summer of 1979, I ended up spending a lot of time with a teammate of mine named John Peasley, probably because we'd long been going down the same path. Up until that time, for as long as I'd known him—if I was an All-American candidate at the nighttime games, he was a Heisman Trophy candidate. We were sure to have a wild summer. Or so I thought.

Except John was different that summer. Way different. He'd gone from being this really angry guy, always looking for a party and a fight, to having a real peace about him. It was just obvious. You couldn't keep from noticing it. I finally just asked him, "What's happened to you, man?"

You can guess. Stop me if you've heard it before, where a guy who's been a rough, tough person, gets tired of the trouble he's causing himself and gets cleaned up to walk the straight and narrow. He tried telling me what he'd experienced, how he'd come to know Christ—how he'd become a Christian—even though the change was still new to him and hard to explain. But I heard him out. And though I didn't exactly admit it then, I got it. I got what he was saying. His description of what had happened to him and the peace that had become so evident and so different in his demeanor made a lot of sense to me. I remember thinking, "You know what? That's what I need." I needed the peace he had.

But I needed to think about it first. And the closer it got to the end of summer, the harder it became to figure out how this desire that I'd been feeling for a new life with God could possibly share space with my old life that would soon be rolling back into town for the fall. What would my roommates think? What would my girlfriend think? What would everybody think? That's what was hanging me up. I was more worried about what people thought than what God thought. Imagine that. Not very smart.

Besides, I still wanted to be a quarterback. So becoming a Christian—especially if it meant being called to be a missionary or something—sure wasn't going to square with what I planned to be doing with my Sundays in the fall.

I knew my identity as a football player wasn't what it used to be anymore. But I didn't know if I really wanted to identify with what being a Christian seemed like to me. I thought it meant being perfect. I thought it meant never doing anything wrong, ever again. And as I took inventory of my sins—and trust me, there were a lot of them—I didn't see how I could ever turn things around without turning into a huge hypocrite. I guess I just didn't understand grace.

I couldn't seem to make that call. Not right then.

Who first told you about Jesus? What role did they play in your faith?

Have you ever experienced a time when you couldn't "make the call?" If so, what got you unstuck?

Are you as close to God as you'd like to be? If not, what steps can you take to bridge the gap?

See group discussion guide for week 1 on page 176.

THE FLORIDA STATE YEARS

DAY 6

Many plans are in a person's heart,
but the LORD's decree will prevail.

PROVERBS 19:21

GOD DIRECTS OUR STEPS

Coming out of college, I think I would've been voted one of the least likely to ever become a coach. For one thing, as a player, I had a bad habit of griping about everything we were made to do. Complaining somehow made all the conditioning feel bearable. Plus, I was always asking questions, questioning what we were doing. Most of it came from a genuine desire to learn. I really wanted to understand why. But I think it just made me seem like a pain in the neck. So how did I get into coaching when it wasn't in my plans?

When I look back to how it felt to be a graduating senior, closing the books on what had been a less than stellar collegiate playing career, I had no idea what to do next. My life had always seemed so clear-cut before. Middle school to high school, high school to college, college to ... now what?

Though I was able to try out for two NFL teams my plans for playing pro football had failed.

But not my steps. God never stops directing our steps. Though "many plans are in a man's heart," as Proverbs 19:21 says, we're not clairvoyant. We don't always know what's best.

I never dressed for an NFL game with an NFL team, even though it'd been my dream from as far back as Boca High, and it remained my dream every day, out on those practice fields all that summer. But here's what I know now that I didn't know then. The same drills that I thought were part of my plan for reaching my NFL dreams were the same drills God was using to plan for my future. The same emphasis on footwork and technique that I thought was part of becoming a professional quarterback was actually how God was training me for becoming a quarterbacks' coach. All those meetings I attended on pass protections and route concepts and timing and delivery—all to make me a better ballplayer, I thought—were the same meetings where God was working to help me become a play caller, a coordinator, eventually a head coach.

In other words, none of that time was wasted, even though none of it took me to the place where I'd been planning to go. Because, again, "the mind of man plans his way, but the LORD directs his steps (Prov. 16:9).

And if I didn't know the truth of that statement yet, I was about to find it out. In a big, big way.

Can you think of a time when you hoped your plans were moving in one direction but your they didn't come to pass? What did you learn?

How has God used your past experiences to help you with a new role?

In what areas are your seeking God's direction for your life?

DAY 7

*Let the favor of the Lord our God be on us;
establish for us the work of our hands—
establish the work of our hands!*

PSALM 90:17

CHANCE OF A LIFETIME

Coaching. It's the first time I'd really pondered it seriously. Coaching? Because I hated thinking I was done with football.

For me, even though I still hadn't given my heart to Christ yet, it did seem my purpose was finally taking shape. I was headed to LSU to be a graduate assistant, slated to work behind Ed Zaunbrecher, their quarterbacks coach. It was a low-level position, but it was a start. It was something. And, hey, it was football. So I packed a U-Haul, finished up my last few pieces of business in Boca, and got ready to pull out the next day for my new life in Louisiana.

Then Coach Bobby Bowden called.

The timing of it was not incidental; it was monumental. It changed everything for me. A true spiritual marker. Because not only did I end up spending all but one of the next fifteen years there with the Florida State football program, working under Coach Bowden, but I met my wife there, Katharyn. Our boys, Jon and David, were born there. We completed the adoption process there that added another son and daughter into our family, Zach and Anya. I met dozens of lifelong friends there. It's just not the kind of thing you could plan no matter how good of a planner you are.

But it's indicative of the kinds of things God can do when He keeps moving us forward each day through things we didn't expect to be experiencing, whether good things or hard things. Somehow He turns them into purposeful things, whether they're exciting or simply mundane. They still serve a purpose. They serve His purpose, His purpose for us. And I'm here to tell you, living out His purpose for us is always better than whatever we would've planned for ourselves if we'd have had complete control over all of it. Following in His steps, where He wants to take us, is what leads us to the people and the places that give our lives their truest sense of meaning and significance.

Man, am I grateful to serve that kind of God, who loved me before I ever gave Him the time of day. He was already directing my steps as a seventeen-year-old kid, back when I first met Coach Bowden on a recruiting visit to Florida State as a promising quarterback, which is likely the only way he would ever have known about me. God had now connected me with a key opening on the FSU staff to work directly under Coach Bowden. Chance of a lifetime. Except that by faith I believe there wasn't anything chancy about it.

So, how did I get into coaching? I believe God took me there.

Can you recall a time when it was apparent God was working in the details of your life?

In what specific circumstances have you learned that God's plans are better than your own?

In what ways would you like to see God work in your career? How might you incorporate these desires into your prayer life?

DAY 8

Never let loyalty and faithfulness leave you.
Tie them around your neck;
write them on the tablet of your heart.
PROVERBS 3:3

CHARACTER MATTERS

Let me just open the door for you here, just for a second, and let you sit in with me on one of my first official meetings with the Florida State University football staff. I'd gotten there in January and had been through spring practice. But that summer I attended what Coach Bowden called his "Hideaway" meeting—the kickoff meeting for the football year.

It was a time for talking with all the coaches about his philosophy, about job descriptions, about the specifics of each person's role, which was especially important for anyone who was new to the program, like me. It was basically a comprehensive presentation on how we would go about our business as a coaching staff, as a football team.

So this was 1985. FSU wasn't quite yet at the place of prominence and dominance that they would eventually attain, where for fourteen straight seasons in the late '80s and throughout the entire decade of the 90s we would post double-digit-winning records and finish in the top five every year. For fourteen years.
Top five. Fourteen years. Think of that.

Here's the culture I walked into as a green, low-paid graduate assistant. Coach Bowden opened the Hideaway meeting with a devotional. Not just a devotional but an explanation of why it was so important that we even have a devotional.

"See, we think we know things," Coach Bowden said. "We're good coaches. We think we know what we're talking about. But we run out of energy. We run out of ideas. We never stop being in need of God's strength and help and wisdom if we're going to be our best at what we do."

With this inspirational lesson as pretext, he then went into a discussion about expectations—what he expected of us; what we could expect of him. Number one was loyalty. No matter how hot the pressures of the season might grow, no matter how loud the criticism might become from outside, he expected a commitment from every one of us to be loyal—loyal to him; loyal to one another. He committed himself to the same thing. He promised to be loyal to us.

Unless. And here was his unless: "If you cheat, I'm not going to be loyal to that. If you cheat, you'll be on your own." Because at Florida State under Coach Bobby Bowden, there was only one way. The right way. And that's what he expected of all the coaches who worked with him. The Bible says, "Dishonest scales are detestable to the LORD, but an accurate weight is his delight" (Prov. 11:1).As believers, we are called to live our lives and conduct our busisness with godly character.

How would you describe what it means to have good character?

What are the benefits of having good character? What are the pitfalls of poor character?

What expectations do you set for yourself? As a leader, what expectations do you set for others?

DAY 9

Don't let anyone despise your youth, but set an example for the believers in speech, in conduct, in love, in faith, and in purity.
1 TIMOTHY 4:12

ENTRUSTING YOUNG LEADERS

1985 was a significant year in my growth as a coach. Art Baker, who'd been the quarterbacks coach and offensive coordinator the year before, had left to become head coach at East Carolina. Coach Bowden added the responsibility of coaching quarterbacks to add to his own responsibilities, but he needed somebody there to help him. So, the way it worked out, he was there to lead me and walk me through the first couple of practices and meetings, but after that, he pretty much left me in charge. Just incredible trust.

Part of being a successful head coach—or a successful leader in any arena of life and work—is found in being able to bring a staff of people together, in motivating them to excellence, then entrusting those who show the heart and ability for it with greater responsibility to carry out the vision you've laid in front of them.

My first opportunity came when we were playing Kansas. Things were going badly. I'm sitting up in the booth, mainly just to feed information to Coach through his headset about the defensive coverages I was seeing. (He was calling the plays himself at that time, from the sideline of course.) And I heard him pause. It was barely perceptible, maybe just a couple of seconds, but enough time to hint that he was feeling a little indecision. And though I was probably out of line to say it, seeing as how I was sitting up there surrounded by a full staff of veteran coaches, I just blurted out: "Red 200 Exxon," a pass play that I thought would work in this third-and-long situation. It ended up scoring a touchdown and turned around a game we were losing.

For me, it was truly a defining moment as a coach. It gave me credibility with Coach Bowden and with the rest of the staff. Even the defensive coaches heard this young kid jumping into the middle of everything. I mean, I was really only a few years older than the quarterbacks I was trying to coach. But in that moment, after feeling the excitement of spotting what to do and then watching it develop and work, right there on the big stage, I suddenly felt older than my twenty-five years. I felt like I'd grown up that day, thanks to a coach humble enough to let a kid sit at the grown-up table like he belonged there, treating even someone like me as if I had a worthwhile role to play.

As Christian men, we're charged with helping other men along no matter their age or inexperience. "Don't let anyone despise your youth," the apostle Paul said to his young ministry protégé Timothy (1 Tim. 4:12). Call them to integrity. Declare to them your loyalty. And give them a voice. Don't be surprised if the whole team becomes better for it.

That's a winning play for any leader.

**Who are the leaders who have guided and taught you?
What did you learn from them?**

What qualities make a good leader?

What motivates you to do your best work?

DAY 10

*For all have sinned and fall
short of the glory of God.*

ROMANS 3:23

THE ULTIMATE CALL

At 2:15 a.m., the phone rang at Coach Bowden's house. The news was terrible—Pablo Lopez, our twenty-one year-old starting left tackle, was DOA at Tallahassee Memorial Hospital—the victim of a gunshot wound. Coach Bowden called a 2:00 meeting for that Sunday afternoon. The whole team. Up in the front row was the first-team offense, sitting quietly in the same assigned seats they always occupied at any team meeting—with one stark, noticeable exception: Pablo's chair was empty.

And Coach Bowden, struggling to hold taut his emotions, pointed wordlessly toward that chair, toward that gap in the heart of his starting unit, before finally coming out with what he'd come there to say. I don't remember it word for word, but it was basically this …

"Men, Pablo used to sit … right there. And none of us, when this weekend started, ever imagined he wouldn't be sitting there in that chair, today. You guys are eighteen, nineteen, twenty, twenty-one, twenty-two years old—you think you're going to live forever, just like Pablo thought. You think it's only old people who die. But look, Pablo's gone. And I'll be honest with you, I don't know where he stood in his faith. I hate that I don't. But let me ask you, if that had been you who had died last night—if it was your chair that sat empty today—do you know where you would spend eternity?"

As soon as he said that—as soon as he posed that question—it hit me like a ton of bricks. Coach told me how to be saved. First thing the next morning, I went to Coach's office to talk with him about it.

He told me how we were all created by God but we'd fallen into sin, how when Adam disobeyed God at the very beginning of time, sin entered all men. All of us. "All have sinned and fall short of the glory of God" (Rom. 3:23). That's a problem for us, because God wants us to live with Him in heaven. But His standard for heaven is perfection. And none of us can be perfect. So we're looking at death and hell forever, with no way out, unless we can somehow be made right with Him.

But God knew this would happen. So God made a way. He sent His Son to live the perfect life we could never live, to die as the perfect sacrifice for the forgiveness of our sins, and be resurrected from the grave. Not even death could keep Him from doing what His Father had sent Him to do.

All we have to do, Coach told me, to receive God's free gift of eternal life is just to believe that Jesus is His Son, our Messiah, and ask Him to be our Lord and Savior. "If you confess with your mouth, 'Jesus as Lord,'" he read to me from Romans 10:9 that morning, "and believe in your heart that God raised him from the dead, you will be saved."

Why do you think some people resist trusting Christ as their Savior?

How did you respond the first time you heard the gospel?

In the simplest terms, how would you describe God's plan for salvation?

See group discussion guide for week 2 on page 178.

DAY 11

For God loved the world in this way:
He gave his one and only Son, so that
everyone who believes in him will
not perish but have eternal life.

JOHN 3:16

A NEW BEGINNING

Everything changed for me when I prayed to receive Christ with Coach Bowden. I didn't know a lot yet about what had happened inside of my heart. I didn't understand, for example, even though he tried to explain it, that I would continue to struggle against the sinful habits that were still in my flesh. I wouldn't walk out of there and never do or think or say anything wrong ever again. I would keep needing Jesus. I still need Jesus. I'll never not need Jesus. But simply by recognizing and repenting of my sins and believing in Him, my spirit and soul became right with God. My heart changed. My desires changed. My way of thinking changed. The things I wanted to be and do … they all changed.

Life became simple for me from that point, as far as my goals and the focus of my life were concerned. I'm not saying life became easy. There's a big difference between simple and easy. But I immediately went from being a selfish guy who only cared about myself, my wants, and my career to being a man who was Christ-centered, who truly wanted to live a life that pleased Him. I went from being that kid who said he believed in football to being a young man who'd found something more permanent to believe in.

It was a tough time for our football team. The toughest. We didn't know if it was something we could get beyond. I'd give anything if it had never happened. But I hope Pablo's family, the people who loved him, as well as all those players and coaches who loved being around him, can hear me say today that Pablo Lopez did not die in vain. The tragic circumstances of his death helped save my life.

It also proves something else: the importance of planting seeds in other people's lives. Because if my college teammate, John Peasley had not been willing to share his faith with me when he did, I'm not sure even the death of Pablo Lopez would've gotten through to me.

I'm grateful God let me live long enough to make the decision He wanted me to make. I'm grateful He gave me time for those seeds to ripen, years after I'd decided I wasn't yet ready to trust Him. I wasn't guaranteed that length of patience. None of us are. I wouldn't be able to make that decision after I was dead. But just as we don't know how long we can wait to get serious about God, we also don't know how timely those little seeds of truth and testimony that we plant in others' lives may turn out to be.

Have you trusted Christ as your Savior? If not, what's holding you back?

If you've trusted Christ as your Savior, how has your life changed since that time?

What seeds are you planting in other people's lives?

DAY 12

*But when you fast, put oil on your
head and wash your face, so that your
fasting isn't obvious to others but to your
Father who is in secret. And your Father
who sees in secret will reward you.*

MATTHEW 6:17-18

A NEW DESIRE

Along with my newfound faith in Christ came a real desire to learn more about Him and grow in my relationship with Him. Many of the things I was feeling and being taught were all new to my way of thinking, and I wanted to know what He truly expected of me.

I became curious about the Christian practice of fasting. I found it interesting that Jesus, in Matthew 6, doesn't say, "If you fast," but "When you fast," where He tells us to do it privately, not for show. Sounds less like a suggestion and more like a command. Having read up on it, I learned it entailed a lot more than just the physical endurance aspect. Fasting involved more than just denying yourself food. The only thing not eating does is make you hungry.

Fasting is a drastic cleansing of your spirit. It opens up your heart more completely to God. You learn a lot about Him in the process. You learn a lot about yourself. It clarifies things you couldn't see before.

I've completed several forty-day fasts in the years since, each for its own specific reason. But the first one I ever did was somewhere during this time period, after I'd been at Florida State for a few years and was seeking direction about what God wanted from me. We were having success, and I was becoming a bigger part of it, little by little, making more contributions to it with each passing season. And that was good. But I wanted to be sure my main goal wasn't getting lost in the pursuit of football glory. My goal now was simply to try living in a way that was pleasing to Christ every day. If that meant coaching football, I would keep coaching football. But if it meant something else—and I truly meant this—I would do something else. But I needed Him to be the One to tell me. I truly wanted Him to be first in my life. Sometimes we need to engage with God through practices like fasting to clarify His desires for us.

What spiritual disciplines do you engage in? (Bible study, prayer, journaling, Scripture memory).

What benefits have you gained from your spiritual practices?

Are there new practices you'd like to try? If so, what steps can you take to implement them in your schedule?

DAY 13

If we confess our sins, he is faithful and righteous to forgive us our sins and to cleanse us from all unrighteousness.

1 JOHN 1:9

HUMILITY AND FORGIVENESS

Fasting brought to mind many sins that I was still allowing to clutter up and complicate my life. Fasting exposed me. It showed me I had a lot in common with that gut of mine, constantly growling to be fed, demanding to be given what it wanted. God showed me in that season of spiritual searching the darkness of my heart, the depths of my pride, the parts of me that didn't want anyone or anything else to be first. Things that needed to be confessed, and then to thank Him for forgiving them at the cross.

It ended up being a truly powerful experience. I came away from those forty days, not hearing His voice in my ears, but definitely sensing Him communicating to me, "I created you, I love you, and all I want is for you to love Me back." Simple as that.

But it was definitely a humbling experience, as I knew it would be. I'd written in my journal on the very first day, "I see fasting as a sign of a person who is trying to humble himself before God." Humility, the Bible says, is the unexpected path to true greatness.

What we somehow fail to realize, because of the persistence of our pride, is that humility is the only path to greatness. Because of our pride we act like glory hounds. But when we follow Christ, He teaches us a new way. The goal is no longer to live for own our achievement. The goal is to live for God and bring glory to Him. It's not easy to do—and we need God's help to live this way. But the apostle Peter wrote, "Humble yourselves, therefore, under the mighty hand of God, so that he may exalt you at the proper time, casting all your cares on him, because he cares about you" (1 Pet. 5:6-7).

Do you make it a habit of confessing your sins to God and thanking Him for His forgiveness? If not, how could you make this a part of your daily schedule?

Why do you think following Christ calls for humility?

Who are the most humble people you know? What stands out about them?

DAY 14

But he gives greater grace. Therefore he says:
God resists the proud but gives
grace to the humble.

JAMES 4:6

GRACE AND SECOND CHANCES

The 1988 Florida State Seminoles, who, based on the previous year's 11-1 record, were being touted as the preseason favorite to win it all. The annual publications were coming out, and the hype and accolades were pouring in. This was supposed to be the year when Florida State, who'd been knocking on the door the past couple of seasons, was poised to knock the door down.

And to somebody—it seemed like this whole Preseason #1 thing was worthy of a "Super Bowl Shuffle"-inspired "Seminole Rap."

Let's hope you haven't seen it, "The Seminole Rap" (though I'm sure you've just now looked it up on YouTube). So, what did you think? Same here. Bad idea from start to finish.

Coach Bowden wasn't exactly a fan of it either, as you'd imagine. But he was an open-minded innovator by nature. And by the time he was made aware of the project, knowing the players had already put work into it and were excited about it, he hated to squash it and dampen their morale. He gave the production his reluctant approval.

I'll go ahead and spoil the ending, if you don't already know it. We went down to Miami for a Labor Day weekend showdown and got our butts kicked, 31-zip.

It was a major come-down for a team that had been pegged as unbeatable and who obviously believed themselves to be. Yet as the Bible says, "God resists the proud but gives grace to the humble" (Jas. 4:6). The path to greatness is not found through thinking ourselves superior to others but by daily just doing our business, keeping a low profile, and quietly believing the truth rather than loudly chanting our own praises.

But here's the thing. This "grace" that God gives to the humble includes the grace of a second chance. He doesn't shame us for becoming enamored with our own write-ups; He loves us enough to catch us on the way down and give us another shot at learning humility on the backside.

How would you explain the concept of grace to a friend?

When has God shown you grace?

Is it difficult for you to extend grace to others? Why or why not?

DAY 15

But grow in the grace and knowledge of our Lord and Savior Jesus Christ. To him be the glory both now and to the day of eternity.

2 PETER 3:18

GROWING FAITH

I asked God to grow my faith; He sent me to East Carolina. Don't take me wrong when I say that. East Carolina has a proud football heritage, emerging onto the radar as a Division I independent under Pat Dye in the 1970s. They love their football, and they'd tasted enough success by then to want to see it grow.

So when they offered me the job as offensive coordinator, it wasn't really a hard call to make. Sure, it was hard walking away from a place that was so established and successful, hard to leave behind the stability and comfort of knowing exactly what was expected of me—the people and processes that I'd become so familiar with. But despite the integral role that Coach Bowden had allowed me to play on his staff, I was still on volunteer status. I wasn't even officially a full-time coach. I'd now be making the leap to coordinator, a big step up for a twenty-eight-year-old.

I quickly accepted.

But I must confess to you, the next day after I'd said yes to head coach Bill Lewis, I called him back and said, "Coach, I hate to do this, but I just don't think I'm ready for the job."

You don't need to be an insider in the world of college football coaching to know that what I'd just done was dangerously close to career suicide. When you get a chance as a young man to upgrade your situation to that extent, you don't immediately start looking for the escape hatch. No matter how overwhelming the responsibility feels, you plow on through the butter-flies. You stop listening to your self-doubts. You get reacquainted with your confidence real fast. You step up into the opportunity that's been provided you. If you don't, word gets around.

I won't go any deeper into how sick my stomach felt or how spooked I'd allowed myself to become at the prospect of being completely in charge of an offense. But to Bill Lewis's credit—and I have a great deal of love and respect for him—he didn't get exasperated with me. If I were him, I probably would've said, hey, "If you don't believe you can do it, maybe I should go find someone else." But he didn't give me that answer. He didn't wince at my indecision. He said, "No, you can do it, Mark. I believe in you."

Okay. I'll do it then.

Often times faith requires we move forward even though we don't know what stepping out will bring. But it's in those steps of faith that we grow in our depen-dence on Christ.

Why does our faith grow in difficult circumstances?

Have you experienced a season of difficulty that matured you spiritually? Is so, what happened?

How would you describe your level of faith in this season of life?

See group discussion guide for week 3 on page 180.

DAY 16

Do not fear, for I am with you;
do not be afraid, for I am your God.
I will strengthen you; I will help you;
I will hold on to you with my
righteous right hand.

ISAIAH 41:10

FAITH OVER FEAR

As things turned out, going to East Carolina actually did become as big a challenge as I'd played it up to be, only not in the way I'd expected. Throughout the first part of this roller coaster ride, the problem wasn't how to run an offense; the problem was whether or not we could get anybody to come lead the defense.

So it was a rough go, a rocky start. Finally a guy named Tom McMahon accepted the job and appeared willing to stay. But even with all the staff movement settled down, the dynamic for me remained tense.

I honestly don't know what I'd have done … If it hadn't been for Katharyn.

We met on a blind date at Florida State, back when I was a grad assistant and she was still a student (though, despite what Wikipedia says, she was not an FSU cheerleader, even though she was certainly athletic enough to be one).

We hit it off and became best friends. I told her all of my darkest secrets, but she liked me anyway. Our friendship grew into a romance, and I asked her to marry me. She said yes. We married in March 1987. I highly recommend becoming best friends before romance and marriage. Two years later, there we were. Alone at East Carolina.

I can say now, that year in the wilderness at East Caro-lina brought me closer to Christ than I'd ever been. And in the midst of a time when I just felt overwhelmed by the challenges I was up against at work, I discovered that if I'd keep repeating to myself the promises of God from the Bible, He would back them up by putting His strength into my spirit. He would keep me from failing. He would deliver me from fear. God and His Word had recalibrated my brain, my decision-making, my emo-tions. I felt, talked, and acted like a whole new man.

In other words, we don't need to turn into super-men in order to gain control over our runaway anxiety. We just need to decide we're going to be driven by faith instead. It doesn't mean everything becomes instantly easy. But it does make life more simple. Instead of fear . . . faith. I found when my faith grew stronger than my fear, I was at peace

What situations are most likely to cause you anxiety?

How might our worries drive us closer to Jesus?

Practically speaking, what does it look like to choose faith over fear?

DAY 17

For me, to live is Christ and to die is gain.
PHILIPPIANS 1:21

WINNING THE BIG ONE

My time in East Carolina came to an end when I got a call from my friend Brad Scott, who I'd worked with at Florida State. He'd called to tell me about some recent developments on Coach Bowden's staff. I was offered a position and we packed our bags. Being back in Tallahassee, coaching quarterbacks, put me in good position to grow, to develop even more in my career.

In 1993, my fourth year back at FSU, we won our first national championship. In our first meeting during the spring of 1994, Coach Bowden was leading the devotional and looked into the faces of all those men, including me, who'd been with him for so long, through so many battles. "They always said we couldn't win the big one. Now we've done it. And here it is, springtime, a couple of months later, and … "

"Mickey," he said, "do you feel any different?"

Mickey Andrews, our defensive coordinator—what a competitor. "No," he said, "not really."

"Chuck? Feel any different?"

"Not really, Coach."

"Billy?"

"No, they just want us to win another championship, is all."

We were getting the picture. Oh, maybe if he'd asked us that same question the day or two after we'd won, we'd have said yes, we did feel different. The night we got back into Tallahassee after our next national championship, I can tell you—Coach's first undefeated season in 1999—I said to Katharyn, as we were heading home from the airport, "Honey, let's go the mall." What for? What do you want? "Nothing. I just want to walk up and down the mall and have people pat me on the back, enjoy what we've done." Yeah, I felt different that night. On top of the world.

But in March? Just working? Trying to rev it all up again?

"No, not really," I said, when Coach called on me to answer. No different.

"Do you know why you don't feel any different?" he said. "Because that's not the big one. Winning the national championship—that's not the big one. The 'big one' is praying to receive Christ as your Lord and Savior. That is winning the big one."

And that is why I loved working for that man.

How would you define what it means to win "the big one?"

**What have you learned from your greatest success?
What have you learned from failure?**

**Why is success empty apart from a relationship
with Jesus?**

DAY 18

*Whatever you do, do it from the heart,
as something done for the Lord and not
for people, knowing that you will receive
the reward of an inheritance from the
Lord. You serve the Lord Christ.*

COLOSSIANS 3:23-24

MY LIFE'S GOAL

I don't know what equates to winning the "big one" in your life. Maybe it's reaching a certain level of employment in your company or becoming a leader in your industry. Maybe it's having a bigger, nicer house than most of your friends. Maybe it's your kid being the star athlete or star whatever that all the other parents wish their kid was like. You tell me. You know what it is.

But none of that, even if it happens, is capable of doing what you always thought it would do. Eventually, you'll come to that "feel any different?" moment, like we did, and you'll have to say, "'No, not really,' because all of those big ones are temporal. They end up being like dust in the wind. Coming to a saving knowledge of Jesus Christ is what's eternal. It's forever.

The Bible says, in what I'd say is my "life verse."

Whatever you do, do your work heartily,
as for the Lord rather than for men.
COLOSSIANS 3:23 (NASB)

I think people tend to get too uptight about what God wants them to do as their life's work. I really believe He is not so concerned about what we do but how we do it and who we do it for. Most of us typically do what we do, not so much to please the Lord, but to please ourselves by pleasing everybody around us. But that's a setup for dissatisfaction. When we do our best and do it for God, I think He loves that.

Also, when we do our work for God rather than men, it's the highest accountability we can have, because we know God is always watching. Even still, we do it out of love for Him, not obligation.

Yeah, we won the national championship that year—the "big one," as the world sees it. That's nice. You and I will often win those kinds of victories when we're doing our very best for God. It's just that they're not enough, all by themselves.

What are your life goals?

**Who are the most important people in your life?
How would you describe your relationship with them?**

**How does your life's work and your relationships bring
glory to God?**

DAY 19

Iron sharpens iron,
and one person sharpens another.
PROVERBS 27:17

KEEP GETTING BETTER

The challenge that comes with being at the top, of course, is maintaining the drive to be your best, to keep getting better. (Maybe that's why that Colossians 3:23 rings so true to me.) When I think about my last seven years at Florida State, moving into the offensive coordinator seat in 1994 after Brad Scott left to become head coach at South Carolina, getting better was the name of the game.

With the people who God had placed around me, it wasn't hard to stay reminded of it. It all started, naturally, with Coach Bowden. Underneath that genuine, folksy, congenial exterior was a tremendously competitive spirit. He was always striving to bring the absolute best out of his players, his coaches, as well as himself.

I don't think it would surprise you to learn, among competitive men, we could sometimes get crossways. Work with a guy long enough, and there'll be moments when you irritate the daylights out of one another. You get to know each other's warts.

But you also know each other's heart—especially when every man, at every morning's staff meeting, is required to take a turn leading a devotional for his fellow coaches. Not everybody was a Christian. You could talk about anything you wanted, as long as it was generally inspirational. But I'd sit there on some days, listening to a guy I'd maybe been angry with, hearing something come out of his mouth, out of his heart, that made me think, okay, "Maybe I don't hate his guts like I did yesterday."

Whenever I talk on leadership, I tell people those staff devotionals that Coach Bowden had us share with one another each morning were the greatest team-building tool of all. It's how we came to trust each other, forgive each other, really know each other. We could still argue our points—and we did! But in the end we were family. We really were. Tough, competitive, but tight-knit, a real team.

Never underestimate the value of your relationships. God intends for us to learn from and invest in the people around us.

Do you view the people around you as people God has chosen to put on your path? Why or why not?

Who inspires you to do your best work?

What leadership traits do you find most valuable?

DAY 20

Trust in the LORD with all your heart,
and do not rely on your own understanding;
in all your ways know him,
and he will make your paths straight.

PROVERBS 3:5-6

LIFE LESSONS AND NEW CHALLENGES

Life is about learning, changing, adjusting, developing. Continuing to put yourself out there and try again. These are the kinds of truths that got burned into my mind over fifteen seasons with Coach Bowden and Florida State.

Lessons about diligence, and determination, and family, and commitment, and listening, and humility, and authenticity, about knowing the difference between the "big one" and the truly Big One. Always getting better. Always doing more. Never settling. Never stopping. Just getting back up and getting back in the game. Getting better, being your best, is often simply the courage (and humility) of learning from your mistakes.

Those are the kind of calls you have to make. On a regular, all-the-time basis. Is today going to be better than yesterday? Will I let past regrets weigh me down so much that I no longer see a future for myself? Have I decided God's gotten tired of me, tired of how I've been living, tired enough that He's finished putting any effort into helping me any more.

Choosing to remain at Florida State had proven a solid decision. I wasn't in a hurry to leave. I loved our players and I loved Coach Bowden. In order for me to think about leaving to become a head coach, it would need to be a special place, somewhere that was awesome for my family and somewhere that I believed the team could win big. By remaining at Florida State, I'd been able to coach another Heisman Trophy candidate, had been able to experience another national championship.

I would need all of those qualities and more for the new level of challenges and responsibility that was soon awaiting me.

What are a few of the most important life lessons you've learned so far?

Why is every morning a new opportunity to choose how you'll live?

Why is it important to make the decision that you'll continue to grow and get better?

See group discussion guide for week 4 on page 182.

THE GEORGIA YEARS

DAY 21

For God has not given us a spirit of fear, but one of power, love, and sound judgment.

2 TIMOTHY 1:7

FEAR IS NOT FROM GOD

As 2000 began winding down, as the coaching carousel began swinging into action, I selectively started listening. In New York that winter, while in town for the Heisman presentation, I met Vince Dooley—former coach and current athletic director for the University of Georgia—for the first time. He asked if I'd be interested in meeting at his room in the Waldorf Astoria, to discuss their head coaching vacancy. I went up with him. Soon thereafter, he invited me to a follow-up meeting with himself as well as the school president, Michael Adams. It seemed to go well.

Still, I wasn't quite prepared when Coach Dooley called the very next day and made me an offer. He'd told me that they had other people to interview. It just caught me off-guard. I thanked him. I told him I appreciated it, but, "Coach, I don't know," I said. "I need to think about it just a little."

This obviously wasn't the response he was anticipating or accustomed to getting. And he was probably right not to expect it. My brother Craig, when I talked with him soon thereafter, said, "What? Are you nuts?" Coach Dooley said he'd be willing to wait until tomorrow, but that was it. "If you don't want this job, I've got to move on, and I've got to move quick."

I knew what accepting the job would mean, the toll it would take on my family, on my health, on everything else. I'd seen the pressure that comes with that position. And though I wanted it, it still scared me. Katharyn knew her Bible, though—how 2 Timothy 1:7 says, "God has not given us a spirit of fear." She said, "Mark, this fear is not coming from God. It's coming from somewhere else. Don't listen to it." I knew she was right. I knew I was just letting myself get carried away. But that's what fear does, you know. It distorts the truth. It shifts all your attention to the costs, shifts it away from the opportunity.

So after wrestling with the decision till about 2:00 or 3:00 in the morning, I finally made up my mind. I was taking it. Then I got concerned that I'd waited too late. I picked up the phone right then—yes, middle of the night—and dialed Coach Dooley's number.

"Coach, it's Mark Richt," I said, "I want the job."

"Uh, good," he said. "That's wonderful. But why are you calling me in the middle of the night?"

"I'm sorry, Coach, I was afraid you might sleep on it and change your mind, so I wanted to catch you before you woke up."

I never get tired of remembering that story. I forged through my fear and found myself working for another great man.

In what areas of your life are you most likely to struggle with fear?

In your experience, how does fear distort reality?

How do the promises found in the Bible equip us to confront fear?

DAY 22

*For the training of the body has limited
benefit, but godliness is beneficial in
every way, since it holds promise for the
present life and also for the life to come.*
1 TIMOTHY 4:8

FINISH THE DRILL

One of the features I brought along with me from Florida State was a Coach Bowden creation known as "mat drills." We did them my first offseason at Georgia in 2001; we did them my last offseason at Georgia in 2015; we did them every year in between. And, trust me, not a single player who ever endured them has ever forgotten them.

Imagine it's about 5:00 in the morning. It's chilly and dark when you arrive at the gym. Everybody's dressed in matching T-shirts and shorts. The whole team sits down on a huge wrestling mat at the center of the room—or most of the team anyway, as many as would fit. The rest sit behind them or around them on the gym floor, everyone in perfectly straight rows and perfectly straight columns, with legs crossed and elbows on knees. Military style.

After a brief time of announcements and warm-ups, you break into three groups: big (offensive and defensive linemen); big skill (tight ends, fullbacks, and linebackers); and skill (QBs, DBs, running backs, receivers). Each group disperses to one of three stations, where they spend twenty nonstop minutes on a series of related drills before rotating to the next station.

One is the form-running station, where you work on movement, core strength, and proper body position.

Another is the agility station, consisting of three different drills: ropes, three-man shuttle, and the "pens," where you perform drills while bent underneath a structure of low-hanging, canvas tarps. No standing up to relieve the screaming muscles in your knees, thighs, and abs. But the toughest of all, both physically and mentally, as well as the toughest in terms of accountability, are the drills run at the mat station. That's why we called the whole program mat drills.

Wave after wave of players come through. The first group's "Go!" is the next group's "Ready!" And if one guy—just one guy—makes a mistake or is dogging it, the whole group goes back and does it again. If one fails, you all fail.

Do it right, do it hard, or do it again.

For a solid hour. Twenty minutes per station. Across all three stations. Without a single stop.

And at every place on the floor, every coach is challenging you: finish every drill.

Finish The Drill!

In our spiritual lives, we may be tempted to give up, but all of us have the strength we need in the Lord to finish the drills He places before us.

How would you describe your level of endurance on difficult tasks?

At what point during a difficult task are you most tempted to quit? What about spiritual tasks?

In what areas do you need encouragement to "finish the drill?"

DAY 23

Let us not get tired of doing good,
for we will reap at the proper
time if we don't give up.
GALATIANS 6:9

REAPING REWARD

Our first, biggest test of the year during my first season at Georgia—after the entire country had been tested by the unprecedented tragedies of September 11—came October 6 on the road against #6 Tennessee. Coach Phillip Fulmer's team, in his tenth season at his alma mater, would flirt again with the national championship. If not for losing to LSU in the SEC title game, they'd have been in the big game again.

So here we go—my first away game as an SEC coach, in front of 107,000 mostly orange-clad fans at Neyland Stadium. They pulled out in front of us early, but the score was tied 17-all heading into the fourth quarter and then things changed.

They led 24-20.

Fifty-seven seconds to go.

Neyland Stadium was literally shaking. The ground was shaking beneath your feet. From where I was standing on the visitor's sidelines, you could feel the tremors disorienting your body. It was pandemonium.

So with ten seconds left, we line up in the I, with Verron Haynes at fullback. Verron, a senior from the Bronx, had been in my doghouse earlier in the year. I'd had to suspend him from the first game. He didn't like that very much. But he'd fought back and become a team captain. And he was about to take a giant leap into Georgia legend.

We faked the run, with Verron blasting toward the middle linebacker, as if to block him, forcing him to come up and look for the ball carrier. But instead of blocking, Verron blew past the linebacker and ran right into the end zone. David Greene, a lefty quarterback, faked the handoff to his right, then twisted his body and floated the ball over the line to Verron, who was waiting all alone. Touchdown.

Wild celebration in the locker room. Here was this first-time coach, this nobody, who most people had never heard of. All of a sudden it looked like my coaching staff and I might know a little something about what we were doing. That game gave us our first big dose of street cred. Much more importantly, of course, it was sweet reward for our players who had worked and hustled and proven their dedication to our football team, all the way back to those dark-thirty mornings in February when they had groaned out of bed and gutted out another cycle around the mats.

After I managed to get the room semi-quiet and had the players' and coaches' attention just long enough to say, "Men, I'm so proud of you," somebody in that sea of Bulldog jerseys—I don't remember who—yelled out, "Coach! We finished the drill!"

That's right. We finished the drill.

How would you describe your work-ethic? Is it as strong as you'd like it to be? If not, what steps can you take to work harder?

Have you experienced a time when working hard over a long period of time yielded results? If so, what happened?

How do you feel when you know you've given your full effort?

DAY 24

Consider it a great joy, my brothers and sisters, whenever you experience various trials, because you know that the testing of your faith produces endurance.

JAMES 1:2-3

FAITH THAT ENDURES

Some teams adopt a different slogan or motto to rally around each season. For us, at Georgia, we had the same one every year. And it all started that day, after that game, when refusing to quit led to one of the great victories in Bulldog history.

"Finish the drill!"

It went on our walls. It went on our T-shirts. It went out into the public, among our fans. Because it's more than just a football lesson; it's a life lesson. It's more than just not quitting on a sports field. It's not quitting on your relationships. Not quitting on your marriage. Not quitting academically or on your job. Not quitting when you're going through a hard time.

I can't tell you how often through the years at Georgia, people would write and ask me to say something encouraging to one of their loved ones who was in the middle of a challenge or crisis, maybe a person who was undergoing cancer treatments or something. I'd say to them nearly every time, "On our team we talk about finishing the drill." I'd encourage them to keep believing, keep hoping, keep working as hard as they could. Then routinely I'd hear how that person decided to make it their little mantra as well. "I'm not gonna quit. I'm gonna be like a Bulldog. I'm gonna finish the drill."

Life calls for perseverance and so does our faith. They'll be times when following Jesus is not easy. They'll be times when the circumstances of our lives seem dark and overwhelming. In some form or fashion, all of us face seasons of hardship that cause us to question, doubt, or even be tempted to give up. But the Book of James says to count these times as a blessing, because hard times purify our faith and only when we are tested do we learn to endure. It's when we're tempted to give up that we learn how to finish the drill.

In what areas of your life are you prone to discouragement?

Thinking about your faith, what keeps you going when you want to give up?

In a practical sense, what would it look like for you to live with the mindset that you'll finish the drill?

DAY 25

Do nothing out of selfish ambition or conceit, but in humility consider others as more important than yourselves. Everyone should look not to his own interests, but rather to the interests of others.

PHILIPPIANS 2:3-4

LOYALTY MATTERS

One of our coaches decided to leave UGA and take what I felt was a lateral move on another staff. Before he moved on, he asked if I would give him one last opportunity to address the players on his side of the ball. Being a young head coach, I thought that was fine, but I said I wanted to be in the room as well.

I'm sure the coach meant what he said to the players that day—how he loved them, how much he'd enjoyed coaching them, how he knew they were each poised to do great things on the football field if they continued to work hard and make the proper sacrifices.

However, as I took the measure of the room, I could sense the hurt that many of them were feeling. You could see it in their countenance, in their body language. "Oh, great. Another guy, walking out on me. More change. More stress." That's the vibe I picked up.

So after the coach had said his piece, I told him I was going to stay behind and speak to the players in private. As soon as we were alone, just the players and me, I said to them, "I want you to know one thing. I'm not going anywhere. I'm staying right here. And I promise you, I will go out and get for you the best coach I can find, a guy who'll come in here and take care of you."

Loyalty matters.

I'm going to sound a little old-school here, I know, but it saddens me to see the painful consequences of disloyalty in our world today. People who didn't keep their promises. People who believed that their own concerns and desires were more important than anybody else's. People who let circumstances, not convictions, determine their decisions. People who chose individual goals over team goals.

When we follow Christ, we put His kingdom over our agenda. People come first. Paul said in Philippians 2:3-4, "Do nothing out of selfish ambition or conceit, but in humility consider others as more important than yourselves. Everyone should look not to his own interests, but rather to the interests of others." Loyalty means that we consider others before ourselves. This posture doesn't come naturally, but is always worth it.

Do you think loyalty is a common trait in modern culture? Why or why not?

In what areas of life do you consider the well-being of others?

Why is it so important to keep our promises?

See group discussion guide for week 5 on page 184.

DAY 26

*For we know that our old self was crucified
with him so that the body ruled by sin
might be rendered powerless so that
we may no longer be enslaved to sin.*

ROMANS 6:6

A WORK IN PROGRESS

Midway through the 2015 season, after suffering back-to-back losses to Alabama and Tennessee, we were struggling at home against Missouri, grinding to a 6-6 tie with about six minutes left to play. Our kicker, Marshall Morgan, after a fourth-quarter drive stalled at the 8, trotted onto the field to attempt a twenty-six-yard field goal from the left hash, for the lead. The ball hooked left.

But after the next series, we got the ball back, giving Marshall another chance. We moved inside our opponent's 20-yard line, fourth and three with 1:48 on the clock. Catching him on his way onto the field, I said, "Marshall," with my arms resting on his shoulder pads, "whether you miss it or make it, you're still my guy, all right? I just want you to know I love you, no matter what happens."

I believe we all need to hear this sometimes—that our performance is not the measure of our worth to God, that we are loved and accepted simply because we are His. As Christians, the moment we agree with God that we are sinners in need of a Savior—the moment we put our faith in Jesus—we become right with God. The sin nature we're born with is "crucified with Him, in order that our body of sin might be done away with" (Romans 6:6). We become a new creation in Christ.

As a result, because we've accepted the gift of Jesus's sacrifice for our sin, we are totally accepted by God. It's not that our sin just magically went away; it's that Jesus paid the price for it. So when we believe in Him, the penalty due for our sin is paid in full. All our guilt, all our punishment, is taken away. We are free.

But even though our spirits have been perfected, our behavior is still a work in progress. Unlike the immediacy of what happens when we receive Christ, the change in our behavior happens over time as we mature in our faith, as we daily begin to understand and experience the changed person God has made us to be.

Again, it's a work in progress. But even though our behavior is not yet perfect, our spirit and soul already are. That's the best news in the world. And that's why we can have peace with God, because we have assurance of our salvation. We can rest from the burden of having to perform to get God's approval.

To put it another way: "You're my guy, Marshall, no matter what happens." Just go out there and kick the dang ball.

He did. We won.

Believers sometimes fail, but we are never failures. We are loved as children of God. That's who we are.

Practically speaking, what does it mean to be a "work in progress?"

Have you ever performed to get God's approval? If so, in what areas? Why is performing unnecessary?

How would your life be different if you lived with an awareness that you are a beloved child of God?

DAY 27

Now to him who is able to do above and beyond all that we ask or think according to the power that works in us—to him be glory in the church and in Christ Jesus to all generations, forever and ever. Amen.

EPHESIANS 3:20-21

OUTSIDE THE BOX

In Jesus, life opens up. For instance, each fall at the University of Georgia, right at the beginning of the semester, they always held a campus-wide pep rally. It was the unofficial kickoff to the school year, scheduled for the Friday before our first home game. As coach, I was usually asked to be one of the speakers, and every year I would use it as an opportunity to say a prayer over the student body—the ones who'd chosen to come that day—asking God to keep them safe, to watch over them, to help them care for one another. Everybody seemed to appreciate that.

There came a year, however, when it looked like I wouldn't be able to do that anymore. One of those activist groups that gets bent out of shape whenever anything slightly religious happens on campus took objection to my public praying—noisy enough that the school administration heard of it, got queasy about it, and decided the blowback wasn't worth it. Without telling me what to do or not do, they kindly got the point across that it might be better all the way around if I just didn't end my speech with a prayer anymore.

Well. Let's see if I really had to live inside that box.

I talked with a constitutional lawyer who knew the legal do's and don'ts of this type of thing. He said, yeah, if you were dealing with high school kids at a mandatory event, you might have yourself a problem. But if your audience is made up of people who are eighteen years of age or older (which it was) and who aren't required to be there (which they weren't), you're well within your legal rights to do all the praying you want, to whoever you want to pray to.

So I could technically do it, but I also knew how our administration felt about it. What should I do? The answer came to me the night before. As I was praying to God, He gave me an idea.

I went to the big event the next day. Hundreds of people in attendance. My turn came to speak, then I reached the part where I would customarily offer my prayer. I said to the group, "Last night before I went to bed, I was thinking about you guys. And I prayed for you. And this is what I prayed for..."

I then told them, not in the form of a prayer but more in the form of a report, exactly what I'd spoken with the Lord about. I mentioned all the things I would ordinarily have addressed directly to Him in their presence. I just didn't say it in a way that could get anybody in trouble for it.

Because believers don't live in a box. Believers get to live in wide, open spaces where everything is possible because our God is truly unlimited.

Are there areas in your life where you feel like your forced to live "inside the box?" If so, what are they?

Have you experienced people or places that are hostile to your faith? If so, how did you respond?

What role does prayer play in your daily life?

DAY 28

After this, the Lord appointed seventy-two others, and he sent them ahead of him in pairs to every town and place where he himself was about to go.

LUKE 10:1

TURNOVERS

I love calling plays. It's a lot of fun. Some of my favorite times in football were as an offensive coordinator at Florida State, sitting up in the booth on game day with the whole field laid out before me.

Then I became a head coach. And the head coach can't spend his whole offseason studying football, studying offenses, studying defenses. He's shaking hands. He's meeting boosters. He's giving interviews. He's raising money. He's on the radio. He's on the speaking circuit. He's on the caravan to neighboring towns and gatherings to sign autographs and smile for selfies. I'm not complaining. I genuinely enjoyed that stuff for the most part because of the people I got to meet in the process. I really did. It's just that football coaches, down in their gut, love football.

And so while I felt blessed beyond words to be head coach at the University of Georgia, I couldn't imagine it getting in the way of what I considered my greatest strengths as a football coach: running the offense, coaching quarterbacks, and calling plays. But there comes a time for each of us, in whatever kind of work we do, that we need to turn some things over … so that we can be our best and so that others can grow.

Jesus modeled this approach. Even though, if anybody ever needed no assistants to turn anything over to, it would be Jesus. He called the right plays at every moment of every day. But He was building a team. He was teaching a new system. He was giving them (and us) a guide for how leaders multiply themselves in those real-life situations where none of us is, you know, God. No matter how good we may be at a certain skill, or at many skills, we humans possess limitations that we ignore at our own peril.

Turnovers are bad in football; turnovers are essential in life.

How do you feel about delegating tasks? Does it make you feel uncomfortable, or do you enjoy giving other people new opportunities to learn?

Who are the key people who helped you grow or learn something new?

Is there a young man in your office or neighborhood who could use your guidance? If so, how might you help?

DAY 29

For if the eagerness is there, the gift is acceptable according to what a person has, not according to what he does not have.

2 CORINTHIANS 8:12

GOD LOOKS AT THE HEART

Sometimes the difference between winning and losing is a matter of feet and inches, of minutes and seconds. In football, you understand that's the way it is. The line is that thin. If you try something that works, you're brilliant. If you try something that doesn't work, you're a bum. Okay. That's fine. That's what we coaches signed up for. But you get good at telling yourself that even if you did everything perfect—there are simply so many things that can intervene to turn a good thing into a bad thing.

A solid play call, no matter how well-schemed, no matter how sound, no matter how creative, can still end up being poorly executed, if not just out-defended by a great defensive player. Even if everybody does their job, you're still playing with a ball that's shaped like an egg. It just bounces funny. Simple physics can either play into your hands or can turn against you. Winning and losing. It's a fine line.

You've got to keep things in perspective. To put it in football language, you can't let a single, isolated loss beat you twice. You can't let negative voices (either your own or other people's) be the only opinions that weigh in on how you did. In many ways, it just gets back to that commitment of keeping things simple. Let's say you come up against a decision that, as you debate how to handle it, your options aren't clear-cut. There are lots of variables and competing considerations that influence how you're going to respond. The difference between choosing well or guessing wrong is not that far apart. You pray about it. You want to do God's will. But even if you do your best to be faithful, you may end up not being so sure you made the right call.

I agree with God's Word that says, "If the eagerness is there, the gift is acceptable" (2 Cor. 8:12). God doesn't look on the outside; He looks on the heart. You go with what you've got, knowing your intention is to please Him, knowing He understands what you're dealing with.

How do you respond when you are unsure about an important decision?

What role does prayer play in your decision-making?

When making an important decision, how mindful are you of pleasing God?

DAY 30

A gentle answer turns away anger,
but a harsh word stirs up wrath.

PROVERBS 15:1

WINNING AND CARING

If there's one comment I heard (and frankly still hear) more than any other, concerning how people saw me as a coach, I'd say it's in that vein of "doesn't show much emotion," "is always on an even keel," "steady," "quiet," "calm." Most people mean it as a compliment, I think. So here's what I'd say to you about that.

First, I'm from Nebraska. If you know anyone from Nebraska, good chance you don't think of them as being super animated. Being calm is just sort of our natural demeanor. I found in coaching, same as I think you'll find in every other walk of life, it's important to be true to who you are. But in my case, staying calm on the sideline was more than just a demeanor. It was deliberate I recognized, as far back as my days as a play caller at Florida State, I made better decisions if my mind wasn't racing. Also, a calm demeanor helps in relationships.

Even when a player was first being recruited, when they were visiting campus, I'd tell them, hey, "When you come to my office, if I invite you into that living room area back there, it means we'll be having a nice visit. If I ask you to sit out here at the table, it means we'll be talking business. But if I tell you to sit in that chair directly across the desk from me, it means you're in trouble." And as I'd sometimes need to remind them later, when I was warning them about things we'd been seeing, I'd say, "Don't let my calm demeanor confuse you into thinking I'm not taking this seriously."

The winning in football is vitally important. I've got no problem with somebody wishing we'd won more games at Georgia, especially wishing that one or more of those wins had been for a national championship. So do I. That would've been sweet. I would also say that by any reasonable measure, a winning record of nearly three to one (74 percent) over the course of fifteen seasons hardly adds up to a less-than-winning culture.

But inside those numbers—as important as they are—nowhere should it be said in college football that relationships come second. Both the winning and the relationships that you build with your players are, in my mind, equally important. I don't buy the notion that a coach can't succeed on Saturday and care deeply about his players' lives every day of the week. I'm okay with that being my lasting reputation. Winning and caring.

And, of course, I say all this in a calm tone of voice.

How would those closest to you describe your communication style?

How does your communication style point others to Jesus?

What steps can you take to communicate more effectively?

See group discussion guide for week 6 on page 186.

THE MIAMI YEARS

DAY 31

*Death and life are in the power
of the tongue, and those who
love it will eat its fruit.*

PROVERBS 18:21

THE POWER OF WORDS

I want to talk about the power of our words. Don't ever believe words aren't powerful. "He who restrains his words has knowledge," the Bible says, "and he who has a cool spirit is a man of understanding" (Prov. 17:27). A cool spirit. I like that. Calm in our character; careful in our communicating. By recognizing and understanding the gravity of our words, we're living out a simple yet profound truth of life, one that we're wise to keep always in front of us.

That's honestly the mindset I took into my final press conference at Georgia, the one where athletic director Greg McGarity formally announced that they were moving on from me and looking to hire my replacement. Even on my way out, I wanted to honor God with how I presented myself. I wanted to show how a Christian man handles this type of situation. From the look on my face to the words that I said, I prayed I'd be able to communicate some important things that would stick with the people who were there and the ones who were watching.

When I talk about every person being a leader in some form or fashion, the rules regarding being mindful about what we say apply to everyone. Parents, for example. If you're a parent, you have ongoing, repeated opportunities for helping to shape the way your child or children think about themselves. All of us can look back on things our parents said to us and how those words impacted our lives, either blessing us or making it harder on us. Words are powerful. They can carry enormous weight.

Each of us has influence. Our words have influence. We can use them to help or to hurt, to build up or tear down. "Death and life are in the power of the tongue," the Bible says (Prov. 18:21). It's up to us whether we use them well or not.

On a scale of 1-10, how mindful are you of the power of your words?

How do you respond when you speak words you regret? Are you quick to apologize and ask for forgiveness? Or do you struggle in that area?

Can you think of a time when someone's words were an encouragement to you? Who needs your encouragement?

DAY 32

The LORD God took the man and placed him in the garden of Eden to work it and watch over it.

GENESIS 2:15

TAKE RESPONSIBILITY

Between 1983 and 2001—a span of only eighteen years—the Miami Hurricanes were national champions five times, quarterbacked by the likes of Bernie Kosar, Vinny Testaverde, Steve Walsh, Gino Toretta, and Ken Dorsey. That's a couple of Heisman Trophy winners in there, surrounded by an incredible cast of players on both sides of the ball. But walking back to the football facility in Coral Gables in December 2016, I was disappointed in what I saw.

One of my first, most telling observations was the sight of a golf cart parked raggedly along the side of the athletic building. It had once been utilized, I assumed, for ferrying recruits from one place to another during official visits. But on this day it just sat there, grass growing up around it, as if it had been there for quite some time, rocked to one side on a flat tire. The tread was worn down to the steel. The inner tube showed. A deflation like that is a process. It takes time. Surely someone should have known it was about to pop and would do something about it, before the grass completely covered the darn thing.

Yet it was pretty much representative of what I saw, to be frank, looking around the facilities for the first time in a long time. Yet where my eyes saw flat tires, my heart saw opportunity. I was introduced with the hope of a new day at Miami, hopefully a return to the glory days.

One night not long after I arrived, I was walking around the campus with a couple of old college teammates, "Right here," I said, "is where we're going to build an indoor practice facility"—the one that people had been wanting and talking about for thirty years but had never been able to get off the ground. We had to have it. We were going to have it.

I'd come to change things. I couldn't do it myself, of course. It would take lots of people, doing a lot of work, investing a lot of support. But I was determined to lead. I was determined to build. To coach and counsel and care for a group of guys who would be part of getting Miami football back on the rails again. God has given each of us spheres of influence and areas of life that we are responsible for. That's what men are made to do. To take care of business.

Are there areas in your home life or career that need your extra time and attention? If so, what are they?

How do you define responsibility?

What responsibilities has God given you in your sphere of influence?

DAY 33

A person's heart plans his way,
but the LORD determines his steps.

PROVERBS 16:9

MANHOOD EQUALS RESPONSIBILITY

My main responsibility at Miami, just like my main responsibility at Georgia, was to win football games. No question. I love winning football. But football, even a winning brand of football, is no more than a four- or five-year slice of life for the players who pass through your program. That's it. And after that for them, it's out into the woods with the wolves of the real world. Part of my job was to get them ready for it.

And so we'd bring people in from time to time, usually early in the spring or summer, in the offseason, to talk about résumé writing, and networking, and dressing for a job interview, and using the right fork at a restaurant. Life skills. As opposed to just football skills. But most of the players weren't ready to listen to all that. As far as they were concerned they were going to the NFL. They'd have a million dollars to help figure all that out, if they ever needed to.

But the vast majority of them, even if they did get to sniff a pro football practice field, would never suit up for a single down. It's hard to make the league. Even if you do, the average career is no more than three-and-a-half years. So the odds are against you. I knew it firsthand. In fact, maybe that's why God took me through those years of failing and being fired, of getting cut and carrying my playbook again to the coach's office. He gave me a heart for how it feels to be on the other side of football, to not know which way is up.

We put a program together at Miami, called the U Network, so that whenever the next player called me, needing help going forward in life, there would be people already in place where they could be directed. Business leaders in the area. Friends of the program. Former players who'd become successful and could reach out with a steady, helping hand, becoming the mentors these young guys really needed at a crossroads moment. And initiating it was as important to me as anything else we were working to accomplish with our ball team.

As was community service. We actually led the nation—#1 among all FBS schools—in the number of hours our players gave to helping people in need. I'd bring in area leaders to talk with our team, maybe as many as five over the course of the offseason, discussing various projects that we could get involved with.

Getting our players out there, where they could see that the world didn't revolve around them, or around football, and that they could find joy in giving to people, was huge in their lives. I wanted them to experience that for themselves. Call it responsibility. Simple as that. It's not something I deserve any credit for. It's just part of what God put men on this earth to do. Manhood equals responsibility.

Do you have a place of service in your church and community? If not, what steps can you take to get involved?

In what areas are you most interested in serving?

How might your life be enriched by serving others?

DAY 34

"His master said to him, 'Well done, good and faithful servant! You were faithful over a few things; I will put you in charge of many things. Share your master's joy.'

MATTHEW 25:23

BE PREPARED

Jesus primarily taught by telling stories. He knows that's how we most easily hear and understand things. Some of His stories gravitated around a similar theme: Be prepared.

He told a story, for example, about ten women who were waiting for a groom to show up for the man's wedding banquet. Because he was slow in arriving, the hour grew late. Five of the women hadn't brought enough oil to keep their lamps burning into the night and had to rush back into town for fresh supplies. While they were gone, the groom arrived. They'd missed him. But the five who'd thought ahead and planned for contingencies were there to welcome him, to be part of his celebration.

The point? Be prepared.

He told another story about a wealthy man who, before leaving on a long journey, gave money to three of his servants and instructed them to put it to good use, that he'd be expecting to see a good return on investment when he got back. Two of them worked to double their money; the third man, because he was afraid to risk losing the money, held back and did nothing with his. Still, the day came when the man returned. The two servants who'd followed their boss's orders brought proof of the profits they'd made; the other man just made excuses.

What's the point? A day is coming when you'll need to show your work.

Be prepared.

Most people watching a football game wonder how a coach decides which play to run on a particular down and distance at a particular moment in the game. They see that big oversized, laminated play card in his hand, with all that tiny writing on it, with all that multitude of options. They hear the announcers offering their opinions on what they think the right play call should be.

Even as a casual fan, maybe you sit there trying to imagine what you'd do. In your mind you know enough to see the potential downside of calling a running play, the possibility of getting stuffed at the line. You also see the downside of attempting a pass, where even more things need to go right for the play to be successful. Pros, cons; opportunities, obstacles.

How do you make the call?

You come prepared.

Think about your greatest responsibilities in life. What does it look like for you to be prepared in those areas?

Describe your current level of preparedness?

What steps can you take to be prepared?

DAY 35

*And let the peace of Christ, to which
you were also called in one body, rule
your hearts. And be thankful.*
COLOSSIANS 3:15

A HARD CALL TO MAKE

Man, was it exciting being part of the resurgence of Miami Hurricane football. But it had definitely taken a toll on me. On my body. On my energy. On my inner reserves and resources. I had never felt so physically, mentally, and emotionally spent in my entire life. I thought I knew what fatigue felt like, but this was a level of fatigue I had never experienced. I was just worn slap out. And it was incredibly disturbing.

I'd been working too hard, too much, and I knew it. Not sleeping enough. Not eating right. Not exercising. But surely I could catch my breath and recharge. I had to. There wasn't any time to slow down. Come on, Mark, let's go. But I had nothing.

Thirty-five years. I'd been doing this for thirty-five years. The twelve-to-fourteen-hour days, seven days a week. The keeping everybody motivated. The building and maintaining of relationships. The constant search for new talent. The constant responsibility for maximizing and maturing the talent you've already got.

On the one hand, I felt an almost all-absorbing duty to fulfill the expectations that I had for myself and for Miami. I also knew if I retired, it would create chaos for every coach and his family. Plus, it would mean leaving the players, which was the last thing I wanted to do. But on the other hand, if I stayed, I knew in my heart it would not be healthy for me, nor would it be in the best interest of the University of Miami.

Have you ever had to make a call like that? You will, if you live long enough. And I promise you, it won't be easy. I mentioned earlier a verse that Christians like to use in helping them sort through tough decisions. "Let the peace of Christ ... rule in your hearts" (Col. 3:15).

Trust Him to lead you to the kinds of choices and solutions that you can be at peace with. But don't think for one second that making hard calls, even for a Christian, is a peaceful experience. You may come to the point of knowing what you need to do, the way I came to it during this process, but don't expect to just follow your sense of peace and let it guide you through. The peace will be there eventually. Peace is there for me now. But there wasn't any peace to be found at the time. I left for my health and for Miami's well-being. It was such a hard call to make.

It doesn't matter the turmoil you feel, the questions that keep you up nights defusing your doubts, fighting to believe. You didn't do what you did because it was easy. And yet somehow, by God's grace, you made it through.

On a scale of 1-10, how well do you take care of your body by getting proper sleep, nutrition, and exercise?

In what areas do you need improvement?

How do you move forward when you have a difficult decision to make?

See group discussion guide for week 7 on page 188.

SUDDEN DEATH

DAY 36

*Do nothing out of selfish ambition or
conceit, but in humility consider others as
more important than yourselves. Everyone
should look not to his own interests,
but rather to the interests of others.*

PHILIPPIANS 2:3-4

ALL THE RIGHT REASONS

By far the hardest part of retiring was knowing that by making my decision, I was making a life-altering decision not only for me and my family but most likely for every man and his family on my coaching staff. When the head coach gets fired, and his staff needs to start looking for other jobs, that's not his fault. Somebody made that decision for him. But when the head coach decides to hang it up himself, when nobody's forcing his hand or pushing him out, he's the one upsetting the apple cart for all the people he's put into place and encouraged to settle their families there.

Plus, it means leaving the players, which was the last thing I wanted to do. But I knew I had to do what was in the best interest of everybody. Like the apostle Paul said in Philippians 2, we have to be mindful of how our choices impact other people. It's not just about us.

The sheer weight of that fallout was nearly enough to make me change my mind, despite not being able to shake what my body was telling me, despite that I was starting to become seriously concerned that something was maybe really wrong with me. The fact that I went ahead with it, against everything my sense of responsibility to those men was pressuring me to do, proves to me just how overwhelming my other reasons were.

I left for my health and for Miami's well-being. That's it. I could've hung around, gone through the motions long enough until everybody else figured out what I already knew, that my physical ability to lead was diminishing. By then, after they'd fired me, my contract would've forced them to pay me millions of dollars not to work.

Instead, I walked out the door myself, leaving millions of dollars behind. But that's what you do when you know you're making the right call. It doesn't matter what it costs you. The calls have to be made. Nobody can make them for you. But you can make them … for all the right reasons.

Have you ever had to make a decision that was costly but you knew it was the right thing to do? If so, what did you learn?

When you make decisions, how mindful are you of how your choices will impact others?

In your estimation, what does it mean to make a decision for "all the right reasons?"

DAY 37

Teach us to number our days carefully
so that we may develop
wisdom in our hearts

PSALM 90:12

TEACH US TO NUMBER OUR DAYS

You've heard of going from zero to sixty. We went from sixty to zero. Katharyn and I had found ourselves settled and happy in our new home on the Florida panhandle, overlooking the gentle surf coming in off the Gulf of Mexico. Most days started now with a morning walk, after which we'd head to the nearby gym for our individual workouts.

It was a Monday, October 21. Not even a year since I'd retired from my life as a head coach and become the talking-head voice of a former head coach. I was home from my weekend on-air duties with the ACC Network, doing what I did every Monday morning now, trying to get my heart rate up. Trying to do a better job of keeping my body well.

There really wasn't much expertise to my old-man workout. I gravitated mostly to the lighter weights, doing higher reps, with not a lot of rest in between. The goal was to keep a little muscle mass and to get my heart pumping, to get the oxygen and blood flow going where it needed to go.

I was preparing to call it a day, when suddenly I just felt like I couldn't catch my breath. I put the weight down, sweating hard, and just sat there trying to recover. I didn't know why I was feeling so unusually overheated. Maybe I'd just overdone it a little. Then I felt a wave of nausea. I huffed over to one of the benches. I had just sat down, then laid down, flat of my back, laboring to breathe, when a scary thought flashed through my mind. Was I having a heart attack?

As Christians, we have no need to fear death but we should be prepared for it. And we need to live every day with the awareness that our time on earth is limited. That's why the psalmist wrote, "Teach us to number our days carefully so that we may develop wisdom in our hearts."

How often do you consider the reality that your time on earth is limited?

What specific things do you want to do with your remaining time on earth?

What would it look like for you to be spiritually and relationally prepared for death?

DAY 38

For me, to live is Christ and to die is gain.
PHILIPPIANS 1:21

THANKFUL FOR HEAVEN

Two EMTs from Sacred Heart Hospital in Miramar Beach—Wes Usher and Richie Frank—were about to go off their shift that morning, just as Luke Turner and Josh Pitts were coming on. So instead of having two guys show up in an ambulance, I got four when the call went out: "Chest pains, sweaty, shortness of breath." Wes told me later that he was almost sure I was going to "code" (hospital slang for "die") right there in the emergency room.

My blood pressure was dropping so precipitously in the operating room that they had to keep me awake instead of putting me all the way under. I was at too much risk. So while Dr. Mayes, the heart surgeon, worked to insert stents into two blocked arteries—both 100 percent blocked, including the left anterior descending artery [LAD], known as the "Widow Maker"—a female nurse sat near my head, repeatedly asking me, "How are you feeling? What are you feeling?"

Everything went numb. Everything went dark. Pitch black. I was thinking, I'm shutting down. I'm dying. This is it.

I don't want to characterize anything that happened next as being anything other than what it was. I won't say it was an out-of-body experience, but in my spirit I was calm, peaceful, even excited to go see Jesus, while at the same time my body was still battling to survive, still gasping for air.

I was dying, wasn't I? I was going to Jesus. I knew it in my head. And, in contrast to the panic I'd been experiencing for the last half hour, I was feeling strangely good. Happy even. I was …

Excited. I'm serious.

I do remember thinking how much I was going to miss Katharyn. I remember that distinctly. But the overwhelming mood and reality that wrapped around me in that moment was a peace and joy and serenity at being ready. Ready to go to Jesus. A thankfulness for heaven. And an excitement. I was truly excited about what lay ahead.

And then …

"Wake up!"

What kind of relationship do you need to have with Jesus now so you will be excited at the prospect of heaven?

If you knew your time on earth was limited, are there any conversations you'd want to have or things you'd need to say?

What holds you back from having these conversations when all is well?

DAY 39

I will thank the LORD with all my heart;
I will declare all your wondrous works.

PSALM 9:1

A LIFESTYLE OF GRATITUDE

That same steady, reassuring voice that earlier had been asking me how I was feeling was suddenly cutting through my calm head space reminding me that my body was still fighting to survive. But at the time, I just realized my body was still fighting to survive.

I think she said something about, "He's got one stent in. He's working on the other"—because apparently, when Dr. Mayes got the Widow Maker open, and could tell I was still in pain, he looked and found the other artery that was blocked as well. That one required three stents. My heart episode had been that serious of an event.

But once all the passages were clear, once the blood started flowing again, that's my first memory of being able to inhale a deep, reviving breath of air. Thank You, Lord. I said. To myself. Or to everybody. I don't know. Thank You, Lord. I could breathe again. I was going to make it. Thank You, Lord.

Often times, we focus on the things we lack rather than all the blessings we have been given. And then we don't realize what we have until we lose it—or come close to losing it. Almost losing your life will make you change your perspective. As Christians, living a lifestyle of gratitude is the only appropriate response to all the blessings we have been given—and the time to be thankful is now. King David said, "I will thank the LORD with all my heart; I will declare all your wondrous works."

Do you think about all the ways God has blessed you, cared for you, provided for you? Have you thanked Him? Do you wake up each morning with a grateful attitude because you have been gifted another day? If not, I encourage you to do so. A lifestyle of gratitude will dramatically improve your outlook.

Do you tend to look at the glass as half-full or half-empty?

How might a grateful heart improve your perspective?

What are specific ways God has been good to you this week? This month? This year? Throughout your life?

DAY 40

Jesus told him, "I am the way, the truth, and the life. No one comes to the Father except through me.

JOHN 14:6

HAVE YOU?

Obviously a medical crises will get your attention. I hope mine has gotten yours. Because in the end, there's only one thing that's important.

What will happen to you when you come to that moment of truth, when there's no deal-making or last-minute cramming that can change the outcome of your eternal destiny? In the end, the only thing that matters is whether you've put your faith in Christ and received His forgiveness of all your sins, or whether you haven't.

Have you?

I'd always known, ever since feeling that wave of conviction in my heart after Pablo's death and praying to receive Christ in Coach Bowden's office—I'd always known it was real. But we're human. We can't help having our doubts. And so on those occasions, like, when an airplane would be rocking with turbulence, and I'd be trying to play it cool though my mind couldn't help realizing that airplanes really do crash and go down, I'd had that question pop into my mind. Am I ready? Am I really ready?

And while I don't recommend having a heart attack, I'm glad today that mine offered me the opportunity to confirm beyond any doubt in my mind that putting my faith in Christ was the right call. I don't know how many minutes or seconds away from death that I came that day, but I do know when I came face to face with end of my life on Earth, I was ready for heaven. Christ had made me ready for heaven.

Christ can make you ready to face eternity.

Only Christ can do that.

I wrote this book because I want to see you in heaven. Putting your faith in Jesus is the way to get there, through the forgiveness of your sins, making you right with God. We can't earn our way; we can't be good enough. We need a Savior, and His name is Jesus.

And so I ask you, just as Coach Bowden put the question to the team after the death of Pablo Lopez: if you had been the one who'd died last night instead of Pablo, do you know where you would spend eternity? It's time to make the call.

Time for you to make the call.

Are you ready to face eternity? Why or why not?

If you haven't trusted Christ as your Savior, what is holding you back?

How would your life be different if you had assurance of what would happen to you when you die?

See group discussion guide for week 8 on page 190.

GROUP GUIDE

GROUP GUIDE 1

Use the following talking points to guide your group discussion. Encourage participants to share highlights from their study time and give group members the opportunity to discuss the follow-up questions.

In this week's study, Coach Richt described in Day One what it means to "Make the Call." He said, "That's the thing about making calls. Sometimes you've got to decide. Right now. You don't have a week or ten days to mull it over. But whether you've got all the time in the world to sit and pray about it, or whether you've got about forty seconds,—you've got to be the one to do it. To make the call."

The Book of Proverbs says:

> *Trust in the LORD with all your heart,*
> *and do not rely on your own understanding;*
> *in all your ways know him,*
> *and he will make your paths straight.*
> PROVERBS 3:5-6

How does the passage above speak to decision-making?

Why is the ability to make decisions such an important characteristic?

What role does your faith play when making decisions?

Do you have any big decisions to make in this season of life? If so, what are they?

Ask God to increase your wisdom and give you the ability to make good decisions. Pray He will give you the knowledge you need to make the right call.

GROUP GUIDE 2

Use the following talking points to guide your group discussion. Encourage participants to share highlights from their study time and give group members the opportunity to discuss the follow-up questions.

In week 2, Coach Richt shared about how his plans to be a professional NFL player changed when God redirected his steps to coaching. He said "It's indicative of the kinds of things God can do when He keeps moving us forward each day through things we didn't expect to be experiencing, whether good things or hard things. Somehow He turns them into purposeful things, whether they're exciting or simply mundane. They still serve a purpose. They serve His purpose, His purpose for us. And I'm here to tell you, living out His purpose for us is always better than whatever we would've planned for ourselves.

Psalm 138:8 says:

> *The LORD will fulfill his purpose for me.*
> *LORD, your faithful love endures forever;*
> *do not abandon the work of your hands.*

How might the above passage serve as a guide for your prayer life?

What challenges do we face when things don't unfold the
way we planned?

Have you experienced a time when God redirected your steps?
If so, what happened and what did you learn?

Pray that God will direct your steps and fulfill His purpose for
your life. Ask Him to guide you to the center of His will and
help you to trust Him when things don't go as planned.

GROUP GUIDE 3

Use the following talking points to guide your group discussion. Encourage participants to share highlights from their study time and give group members the opportunity to discuss the follow-up questions.

In week 3, Coach Richt explained how everything changed for him after he trusted Christ as his Savior. He said, "Everything changed for me when I prayed to receive Christ with Coach Bowden right there in his office. I didn't know a lot yet about what had happened inside of my heart. I didn't understand, for example, even though he tried to explain it, that I would continue to struggle against the sinful habits that were still in my flesh. I wouldn't walk out of there and never do or think or say anything wrong ever again. I would keep needing Jesus. I still need Jesus. I'll never not need Jesus. But by believing in Him, simply by recognizing and repenting of my sins and believing in Him, my heart changed. My desires changed. My way of thinking changed. The things I wanted to be and do changed."

What Coach Richt is describing here is what it means to be a new creation in Christ. The apostle Paul wrote, "Therefore, if anyone is in Christ, he is a new creation; the old has passed away, and see, the new has come!" (2 Cor. 5:17).

Do you remember the moment you trusted Christ as your Savior? If so, what happened?

How has Christ changed your heart?

Coach Richt said, "I would keep needing Jesus. I still need Jesus." How would you explain your need for Jesus?

> Ask God to align your heart with His. Pray that He will change your thinking and desires so they reflect His will. Pray you will be continually mindful of how much you need Jesus.

GROUP GUIDE 4

Use the following talking points to guide your group discussion. Encourage participants to share highlights from their study time and give group members the opportunity to discuss the follow-up questions.

In week 4, Coach Richt described a time of extreme anxiety that brought him closer to Christ than he'd ever been. He said, "I discovered that if I'd keep repeating to myself the promises of God from the Bible, He would back them up by putting His strength into my spirit. He would deliver me from fear. God and His Word had recalibrated my brain, my decision-making, my emotions. In other words, we don't need to turn into supermen in order to gain control over our runaway anxiety. We just need to decide we're going to be driven by faith instead."

Second Timothy 1:7 says:

"For God has not given us a spirit of fear,
but one of power, love, and sound judgment."

What specific areas cause you fear and worry? How does this passage speak to your struggles?

Coach Richt described how the Word of God helped him with worry and anxiety. Are there specific passages of Scripture you lean on when you are worried? If so, what are they?

What would your life look like if you chose to be driven by faith instead of fear?

Ask God to increase your love for His Word. Pray He will help you confront fear by relying on HIs promises.

GROUP GUIDE 5

Use the following talking points to guide your group discussion. Encourage participants to share highlights from their study time and give group members the opportunity to discuss the follow-up questions.

In week 5, Coach Richt describe what it meant for his team to "Finish the Drill." He said, "It went on our walls. It went on our T-shirts. It went out into the public, among our fans. Because it's more than just a football lesson; it's a life lesson. It's more than just not quitting on a sports field. It's not quitting on your relationships. Not quitting on your marriage. Not quitting academically or on your job. Not quitting when you're going through a hard time."

First Corinthians 13:7 says:

> *[Love] bears all things, believes all things,*
> *hopes all things, endures all things.*

How does this verse relate to "Finishing the Drill?"

Are there areas in your life where you are tempted to quit?
If so, what are they?

What does it look like for you to "Finish the Drill" in your specific
circumstances?

Ask God to give you perseverance to finish your tasks. Pray you will
have the spirit of self-control that allows you to "finish the drill."

GROUP GUIDE 6

Use the following talking points to guide your group discussion. Encourage participants to share highlights from their study time and give group members the opportunity to discuss the follow-up questions.

In week 6, Coach Richt talks about how to respond when things don't go the way you hoped. He said, "A solid play call, no matter how well-schemed, no matter how sound, no matter how creative, can still end up being poorly executed, if not just out-defended by a great defensive player. It's true in football and it's true in life. The difference between choosing well or guessing wrong is not that far apart. You pray about it. You want to do God's will. But even if you do your best to be faithful, you may end up not being so sure you made the right call."

Proverbs 11:14 says:

Without guidance, a people will fall,
but with many counselors there is deliverance.

How do you move forward when you aren't sure what the right call is?

Who are the people you turn to for advice?

What is the godly way to respond when things don't turn out like you hoped?

Pray that God will be quick to redirect your steps when you get off-track. Ask Him to surround you with wise counsel. Ask Him to help you respond in a godly manner when things don't go the way you hoped.

GROUP GUIDE 7

Use the following talking points to guide your group discussion. Encourage participants to share highlights from their study time and give group members the opportunity to discuss the follow-up questions.

In week 7, Coach Richt talks about the power of words. He said, "By recognizing and understanding the gravity of our words, we're living out a simple yet profound truth of life, one that we're wise to keep always in front of us. That's honestly the mind-set I took into my final press conference at Georgia. Even on my way out, I wanted to honor God with how I presented myself. I wanted to show how a Christian man handles this type of situation. From the look on my face to the words that I said, I prayed I'd be able to communicate some important things that would stick with the people who were there and the ones who were watching.

Proverbs 18:21 says:

> *"Death and life are in the power of the tongue,*
> *and those who love it will eat its fruit."*

How does this passage influence how you want to choose your words?

How would those closest to you describe your speech?

In what areas are you most likely to sin in your speech?

When are you most likely to say something you'll regret?
How can you be prepared for these instances?

Ask God to help you to choose your words wisely. Pray you will speak words that help and encourage people.

GROUP GUIDE 8

Use the following talking points to guide your group discussion. Encourage participants to share highlights from their study time and give group members the opportunity to discuss the follow-up questions.

In week 8, Coach Richt talked about his close call with death. He said, "I don't recommend having a heart attack, I'm glad today that mine offered me the opportunity to confirm any doubt in my mind that putting my faith in Christ was the right call. I don't know how many minutes or seconds away from death that I came that day, but I do know when I came face to face with end of my life on Earth, I was ready for heaven. Christ had made me ready for heaven. Christ can make you ready to face eternity.

Only Christ can do that. What will happen to you when you come to that moment of truth, when there's no deal-making or last-minute cramming that can change the outcome of your eternal destiny? In the end, the only thing that matters is whether you've put your faith in Christ and received His forgiveness of all your sins, or whether you haven't."

Romans 10:9 says,

> *"If you confess with your mouth, 'Jesus is Lord,'*
> *and believe in your heart that God raised*
> *him from the dead, you will be saved."*